HELL IS REAL

Hell is Real

An Eyewitness Account

Steve Yates

Copyright © 2009 by Steve Yates.

Library of Congress Control Number:		2009912131
ISBN:	Hardcover	978-1-4500-0032-1
	Softcover	978-1-4500-0031-4
	Ebook	978-1-4500-0033-8

All rights reserved solely by the author. The author guarantees all contents are original and do not infringe upon the legal rights of any other person or work. This book or parts thereof may not be reproduced in any form, stored in a retrieval system, or transmitted in any form by any means—electronic, mechanical, photocopy, recording, or otherwise—without prior written permission of the author, except as provided by United States of America copyright law. The views expressed in this book are not necessarily those of the publisher.

All scripture references are taken from the King James Version of the Bible unless otherwise noted.

This book was printed in the United States of America.
To order additional copies of this book, contact:
Xlibris Corporation
1-888-795-4274
www.Xlibris.com
Orders@Xlibris.com

Contents

Preface 11

Chapter 1	From Darkness to Light 15
Chapter 2	Satan's Great Lie 25
Chapter 3	The Sea of Souls 41
Chapter 4	The First Great Torment: Fire 57
Chapter 5	The Second Great Torment: The Memory of Man 67
Chapter 6	The Third Great Torment:
	The Sense of Utter Hopelessness 75
Chapter 7	Common Mistakes and Misunderstandings About Hell . 81
Chapter 8	Hell Can Be Avoided 99

Endnotes 105

To my wife Chineta for always believing in me. To my children, Dustin, Justice, Cali and Faith, your love and faith in God inspires my own. To Tommy Leaks, a friend who is constant and faithful and without whom this book would never be published. Thanks be to God, for revealing His great mysteries to mankind. May this book glorify your Name.

Preface

People from all times and ages were standing around me but I did not care to look . . . I did not care, and neither did they, because we were burning in the flames.

This book is the result of my dedicating a number of years to studying the scriptures in order to either refute or substantiate what I had both seen and heard during my time in hell. Thus, I will provide scriptural background for what I experienced. I learned many important truths about the nature of the mind, spirit, and body while in hell, and I will share many of them as I chronicle my eyewitness account. This is not a work of fiction.

One of the greatest difficulties I encountered while writing this book was trying to retell the occurrence exactly the way I experienced it. What I am about to recount did not occur as a linear event, where one thing happened and then the next. Rather, the experience was immediate and instantaneous and completely enveloping.

Think of a worker at an outdoor carnival sitting in a water cage. My experience was akin to when the ball strikes the target. The worker hears the sound of the bull's eye's metal arm being triggered as he plunges into the water, and although totally immersed in his watery environment, his sight, emotions, and feelings explode with activity. All of his senses are working and recording the events exactly as they unfold. Like a palette of many colors, his senses are working flawlessly and independently, yet as one, cooperating to produce a single image of exactly what is taking place. My awareness of the situation was total and its torments painted clearly for me.

Like others who have encountered the awesome complexities of the supernatural, I am forced to use analogies to help the reader picture the event. For example, John, while recording his visions in the Book of Revelation, wrote that Jesus' hair was *like* wool, and His feet *like* fine brass, etc. To that end, I will use many common illustrations to explain my visitation to hell—with this one caveat: no adjective, metaphor, or analogy the English language can provide could adequately capture what I witnessed.

I experienced everything a human soul would while suffering from hell's torments. However, what I am going to attempt to describe is not meant to imply that the aspects of my encounter encompass all there is to know about hell. I will only relay those particular occurrences and truths that became unmistakably apparent to me while I experienced them. Further, because I was not there as an observer but as a participant, it is impossible for me to give a detailed description of all the particular aspects of hell.

The truth is, when I was burning in the flames, what should have been important to take note of as an observer in hell, I found no interest in at all. No sight, no sound, and no location carried any importance. Before my experience, I always assumed that, at the very least, there might be some tinge of desire to take a look around my surroundings in an effort to prepare myself for where I would be spending eternity. Those conventional thoughts are for those who have never been there.

It is expected that some will not believe my account, but it is not my purpose to make anyone believe. It is, however, my desire to impart the truth about hell, as the Lord has revealed these truths to me. Yet, the Lord has given me an even greater responsibility: *to relay the message*. All must prayerfully do with that message as their hearts lead.

Why Me?

Since experiencing my vision, I have been asked one question repeatedly: Why do you think God showed hell to you? There's no easy answer, but to put it as simply as I can, my response is, *because I asked.* No, I didn't ask God to send me to hell, but I did put this request to Him: "God, if I am headed on my way to hell and don't know it, at least don't let me go without knowing the Truth!"

Look at it this way. What would you want to know if you were standing before a two-ton nuclear bomb, the seconds ticking away, and a million lives, including yours, were at stake? Answer: How do I stop the destruction! I didn't wish to go to hell, but I did want to be armed with the information necessary to avert my own total destruction.

Here are the circumstances that prompted that question.

Chapter 1

From Darkness to Light

I was an ex-gang member from Cincinnati, Ohio, with a history of family troubles and anger management problems (to put it lightly). Because of these, I dealt with people in violent ways. Instead of allowing myself to be afraid of others or try to articulate my thoughts and feelings to someone who disagreed with me, I would rather fight them, and thus cut through the unnecessary pretense. Unfortunately, that violent lifestyle caught up with me in June of 1989.

Within a month after graduating from high school, I was involved in a physical altercation in which I was stabbed in the throat and almost died. Fearing for my life, I gathered a trash bag full of clothes, left my home and the streets of Cincinnati, and moved to Columbus, Ohio, two hours away. While contemplating my next move, a childhood friend, who had recently moved to Florida to go to school at Florida A&M University, encouraged me by saying, "Steve, I believe that if you can get down to Florida and go to school, your life will change!"

At that time, *Miami Vice* was big on television, and all I could imagine Florida to be was a place filled with beautiful women and tall green palm trees. It wasn't long before I was cruising my gray Volkswagen Rabbit down Interstate 75 to Florida to live. Although my heart had been hardened through years of rough living, I was still looking forward to leaving behind the life I had led. I enrolled immediately at the university and found an apartment within walking distance of the school. I was excited! I was in a new place, I was making a new change, and I was in a college town with other people my age who were trying to make something of themselves.

After settling into my apartment, I met some neighbors who were in school like me, and we started hanging out. Whenever they partied, I partied, where they went, I went, and whatever they drank, I drank. I was living a life without conscience or restraint. Despite the change of location, inwardly I remained the same Steven Yates. To be honest, I had gotten even colder and more selfish than ever before. I trusted no one.

Needless to say, at this point in my life I was not a Christian, and even though I had attended church in my youth, I had never personally read a Bible or believed in Christ. Around my twelfth birthday, my father gave me the choice of whether to attend church or not. I guess he was tired of all the fussing and grumbling my sister and brother and I made him put up with every Sunday morning. To me church was boring, so it was with little hesitation that I decided not to go again. It would be another six years before I entered another church building. Although as a little child I had believed there was a God, as I got older, I drifted farther and farther away from that tenet. I had come to believe that there *may* be a God, but that there was absolutely no way we could get in touch with Him or know Him to be real for sure. I learned later that the term for my position was *agnostic*.

Shortly after arriving in Tallahassee, Florida, I met a girl at a party and we started dating. When she asked me to go to church with her I went reluctantly, not wanting to create a strain on a newly formed relationship. She wasn't a Christian at the time, but like many of our friends, she only went to church to see who had the audacity to show up at the service on Sunday morning after they'd partied at the club Saturday night.

Well, before I'd even gotten my feet wet in my new life, God touched my heart in the first church service I attended, through the first sermon I'd ever heard, and after the first invitation I'd ever heard to receive Jesus in my heart. I had grown up listening to passionless liturgies given by Catholic priests, but this was my first sermon preached by a full-blown Baptist preacher! When he gave the altar call my heart was pricked about the sin in my life, and I became aware that God was asking me for the first time to turn my life over to Him fully. I had always been a person who valued one's commitments, so I knew if I were going to commit my life to God it would be forever. I thought about how my decision probably meant I would lose my new friends, but I counted the cost, and a week later, I gave my life to Jesus Christ.

The Great Dream

In addition to the fear of losing my friends, I harbored another fear: that I was going to have to give up the lifestyle I had grown so comfortable with. I worried God was going to make me vulnerable to those people who were as mean as I was. Who would like me then? None of my friends ever talked to me about Jesus, but now I would have to let them know what I'd decided to do. But to my surprise, after telling a couple of my friends about my conversion, I found out that the people I had been partying with were Christians already!

What a revelation! What liberation! All the people I drank with, cussed with, and partied with were all Christians! This came as awesome news to me. These people whom I'd been having so much fun with as an unbeliever were what I thought real Christians were like!

You have to understand. Up to this point, without having read the Bible, my only role models of what Jesus would do were my friends who *called* themselves Christians. I said to myself, *You mean to tell me, all this time I've been running from God, thinking I would have to change my life in order be able to go to heaven, and all these things I had considered sinful are what Christians can do? Man, if I'd known that, I would have given my life to Christ a long time ago!*

For the next several months, it was like I'd been given an official license to sin. I was not only a member, but I was the president of the club. During this time, I was given a little blue King James Version of the Bible. I faithfully carried it to church every Sunday, and faithfully put it back in the same spot every Sunday evening. My Bible was so unused, when you tried to open it the crisp pages sounded like someone was eating potato chips. At the time, I had no reason to believe that what my friends or I were doing was wrong. I even did things after I was converted that I am now ashamed of, because I honestly didn't know they were wrong, and none of the Christians around me told me anything different.

I soon joined the church most of my friends attended and saw how some of the wildest of us had no problem living in both worlds. As for me, I was happy to tell certain people I was a Christian man, because my admission would rack up points in the dating game. The life I once lived, and the life I'd just received were now so intertwined you couldn't tell the difference between them. And quite frankly, I had no problem with that. I was completely immersed in a carnal lifestyle, born again but without any understanding or teaching from the Bible. I was on my way to destruction, and I had no one to instruct me!

My people are destroyed for lack of knowledge (Hosea 4:6).

I really thought that Christianity was as good as my own version of it got. In my brand of Christianity, there was no power, no healing, no miracles, no change, and *no conviction*. This is where the Lord decided to mercifully intervene and visited me in a dream.

One night, after settling into bed, I drifted off to sleep and began to dream. I found myself walking across the college campus I was attending, when suddenly, as I passed by the main library; the overwhelming presence of God engulfed me. As I looked around, I saw that students all across the university were experiencing what I was. Everyone stopped moving under God's powerful presence. There was no mistaking what was happening; God had come to reclaim the earth.

As I gazed around, I saw self-proclaimed atheists, agnostics, and people from all different religions, who had denied Christ before. Suddenly, they all were falling to the ground weeping for mercy from God. I remember thinking it was so hypocritical that these same people, who had just fallen to their knees, had preached there was no God, and yet now they were crying out to Him.

Before long I was the only one standing. Suddenly I felt a strong conviction overtake me. I became intimately aware of the deep sin in my own life, so I decided, at the very least, to do what I saw everybody else doing. I dropped to my knees, and just to make sure I did my part, almost mechanically I began to rattle off my sins. It was then I saw what looked like fiery rocks fall from the sky and consume people, one after another.

Soon the whole campus was ablaze. I looked up into the sky and saw a massive hand reach out of a cloud and pull me up into the sky. I was now facing the fire-consumed campus, and a bellowing voice spoke out of the cloud, "You said to me that in the day of My coming, you would be ready and have no need to offer prayer as other people are doing this day because you would be justified. But you, like the others, have knelt down to pray to me because you are not ready. Now, therefore I say to you, you shall suffer as they because you were one that heard and knew the truth to be prepared but took no heed to the warning!" And then the hand flung me back into the flames.

Needless to say, I awoke and sat straight up on my bed in my room, terrified by what I had just witnessed. At that moment I had my first encounter with the voice of God. I heard an audible voice speak to me out of the darkness of my room and say, *"Steven, you don't know Me. READ MY WORD!"* I almost fell off the bed, racing to get to my Bible. I didn't care *what* I read or *where* I read, I just knew I needed to *read*. I opened the Bible for the first time. Remarkably, I opened to Philippians 2:9-11: *Wherefore God also hath highly exalted Him, and given Him a name which is above every name: That at the name of Jesus every knee should bow, of things in heaven, and things in earth, and things under the earth; And that every tongue should confess that Jesus Christ is Lord, to the glory of God the Father . . . .*

As I finished reading the last words, a tremendous sense of awe flooded my soul. It was as if I were reliving the dream all over again. Possibilities and questions seemed to explode in my mind. *God has called me by name and wants me to know Him? You mean, He actually cares how my life ends up?*

I knew from that moment on that God speaks to men. He'd called me by my name and then showed me a graphic illustration from passages right out of the Bible! I fell down on my knees in the middle of my apartment, and I still remember the honest prayer I prayed that night. I said, *God, these pages are too thin, and the words are too small, and this book is too thick, but if You help me, I will read it all.*

My Life Changes

As if to supplant the first feeble months of my Christianity, God gave me an insatiable hunger for His Word. I would read non-stop day in and day out. I read so much that I began to speak to people in King James English!

I lived every day as if it were my last. Every night was an opportunity to read more about Him. Night after night, I would go outside and look up at the stars, wondering if this was the night He was coming back. My neighbors used to look at me real funny in those days, glory to God! Standing outside stargazing may have seemed strange, but it kept me seeking God.

> *Keep yourselves in the love of God, looking for the mercy of our Lord Jesus Christ unto eternal life. And of some have compassion, making a difference: And others save with fear, pulling them out of the fire; hating even the garment spotted by the flesh*
> (Jude 1:21-23).

The more I learned about God, the worse I felt about how I had been living without truly knowing Him. I realized I needed to change. More significantly, I realized I had been emulating other people's dubious relationships with Christ and not seeking to know Him for myself.

Looking back at my ignorance, I realize there came a time when I prayed a prayer that I believe is the reason God has since given me this vision and many other wonderful experiences. I prayed, "God, I realize I was on my way to hell. If I am ever headed down the road to hell, don't let me go without *at least* knowing the Truth!" At the time, that was my sincere attempt at asking God to give me a chance to know for myself what was right, and then be able to choose which path I would walk. If God answered this prayer, I would never be led astray through ignorance and still be punished for it. I wanted to take responsibility and ownership for my own decisions and have the opportunity to decide to live for Christ.

Since then, God has honored my heartfelt prayer time and time again, and has shown me many wonderful things, both in the spirit and in his Word. God knew all along how I would react to His revelations. He also knew I would write this book, and that right at this moment you would be holding it in your hands. If anyone reading these words can identify with what I have written so far, either for yourself or someone else you know, then I believe God wants you also to know the truth about the penalties of living without Him—so that while we still have time we can enjoy the pleasures of living with Him!

Chapter 2

Satan's Great Lie

The wwicked shall be turned into Hell, and all the nations that forget God (Psalm 9:17).

For years, both television and cartoons have painted my concepts of hell for me. I remember watching an old *Tom and Jerry* episode where the living room floor opens up under Tom's feet and he falls down into hell. The cartoonists illustrated hell as a place where Tom's worst enemy, now transformed into a maniacally laughing Devil Dog, uses his pitchfork to prick and shove the screaming and yelping Tom down into a searing pot of flames.

From early on, I've always heard the devil spoken of synonymously with hell. I had honestly come to imagine that hell was a place, like a kingdom, where Satan ruled with his demons, and where people were tortured for their sins. Sound familiar? I had even read a book that described hell as a place filled with demonic jailers and demonic carnivals where the condemned could torture those in death who'd tortured them in life.

Our opinions are formed by what we see and hear, whether we are conscious of that fact or not. I believe the wide misconception of hell has been exacerbated due to a lack of proper teaching. Popular media has also played a large part in diluting any real or accurate biblical concept of hell. Unfortunately for the Christian church, rarely, if ever, do we hear hell being preached. Why is this? Are we trying to compensate for the many years of misguided emphasis on hell, until today we can offer no educated emphasis on it at all? There must be a balance! If God said it in His Word, then it is meant to be repeated! Glory to God!

What Hell Is Not

I believe that the enemy desires to suppress accurate knowledge about the reality of hell. He's placed himself in position to paint an incorrect image of hell for us, an image that may somehow appear tolerable, if at the same time horrific and scary. Unfortunately, this method has fooled some hardened people into believing that if they end up in hell, they might have been bad enough on earth to gain a name or position there.

One former Satanist-turned-Christian pastor, when writing on the faulty thinking of many young Satanists, stated, "They suppose Hell will only be a place of torment for those who do not serve Satan on earth. For those who do, it will be an endless party."[1] Others have tragically assumed that if they die in their sinful lifestyle, hell could offer no greater suffering because they have already suffered so much in life. This false sense of comfort is exactly what the enemy wants to sow in our hearts. He wants to blind us so that we may be blinded to the simple truths of Scripture, and hopefully convince us that hell is not what the Bible declares it to be.

From my hellish visitation, I quickly learned that what I had been conditioned to believe was nothing like the actual reality of hell or its torments. I witnessed that the torments of hell are not brought on by evil spirits, or even by Satan himself. I found the best description of hell's torments in the story of the condemned rich man.

> *And in Hell he lifted up his eyes, being in torments, and seeth Abraham afar off, and Lazarus in his bosom. And he cried and said, Father Abraham, have mercy on me, and send Lazarus, that he may dip the tip of his finger in water, and cool my tongue; for I am tormented in this flame* (Luke 16:23, 24).

Had you ever considered the scriptural account of the rich man's sufferings? Had you noticed that it was flames that tormented him and not devils? It was not until after my experience that I understood the importance of this passage of scripture. The scriptures declare that God created only one thing for the devil, and that was fire! Jesus said, *Depart from me, ye cursed, into everlasting fire, prepared for the devil and his angels* (Matthew 25:41).

Hell's fire was originally created as an instrument of God's judgment for both Satan and those angels that followed him into banishment from heaven.

> *God spared not the angels that sinned, but cast them down into hell and delivered them into chains of darkness, to be reserved*
> *unto judgment . . .* (2 Peter 2:4).

Where Is Satan's Kingdom?

To some this may come as a shock: *Satan is not in hell*. God is in control of everything, even hell, because hell is His place of judgment, not Satan's throne of power!

> *And fear not them, which kill the body, but are able to kill the soul: but rather fear Him, which is able to destroy both soul and body in Hell* (Matthew 10:28).

Jesus is not talking about the devil having this power, but rather instructing us to fear God and not man. In the scriptures, the devil's location of authority has always been identified. Since the time Satan and his demons were cast out of heaven, earth has been their residence (Ezekiel 28:16-17).

> *And the great dragon was cast out, that old serpent, called the Devil, and Satan, which deceiveth the whole world: he was cast out into the earth, and his angels were cast out with him* (Revelation 12:19).

Jesus describes Satan as the prince of this world (John 14:29-30), and Paul calls him a god of this world (2 Corinthians 4:3-4). Paul further says that the struggles we face as humans are the direct result of the fact that demons dwell here on earth, roaming to and fro exercising their anger. Paul says in Ephesians 6:12, *For we wrestle not against flesh and blood, but against principalities [princes over lands], against powers, against the rulers of the darkness of this world, against spiritual wickedness in high places.* Indeed, we find in the scriptures that Jesus said that fallen angels called "demons" are inclined to reside in people.

> *When the unclean spirit is gone out of a man, he walketh through dry places, seeking rest, and findeth none. Then he saith, I will return into my house from whence I came out; and when he is come, he findeth it empty, swept, and garnished. Then goeth he, and taketh with himself seven other spirits more wicked than himself, and they enter in and dwell there: and the last state of that man is worse than the first* (Matthew 12:43-45).

Satan also hates all of God's creation, so he continually wages a diabolical war against all of nature. Animals are also a secondary place of residence for evil spirits.

> *And when he was come to the other side into the country of the Gergesenes, there met Him two possessed with devils, coming out of the tombs, exceeding fierce, so that no man might pass by that way. And, behold, they cried out, saying, what have we to do with thee, Jesus, thou Son of God? Art thou come hither to torment us before the time? And there was a good way off from them an herd of many swine feeding. So the devils besought Him, saying, If thou cast us out, suffer us to go away into the herd of swine* (Matthew 8:28-31).

Yes, evidence is found throughout the Bible that Satan makes people, places, and things his habitations. So you see, hell has been reserved as a place of punishment for Satan when his tyranny on earth comes to an end.

Unfortunately, after the fall of Adam, that punishment also included those of mankind who chose to follow Satan and his ways. Satan does not want to be alone in his doomed future. Thus, the apostle Peter sent a warning to believers in Christ: *Be sober, be vigilant; because your adversary the devil, as a roaring lion, walketh about, seeking whom he may devour. Whom resist stedfast in the faith, knowing that the same afflictions are accomplished in your brethren that are in the world* (1 Peter 5: 8-9).

Since the beginning, at his fateful encounter with Eve, Satan has sought to deceive God's children about the consequences of sin. Lewis Drummond, in his book, *The Evangelist*, writes when describing the effects of sin on an unwitting world, "One of the most devastating effects of human sin resides in its ability by Satan to blind people to its destructiveness."[2] If you think that those who end up in hell are hapless victims of a vengeful God, think again. All those who suffer hell's fate have one thing in common: They all chose to live their lives contrary to the way God intended. It is that life of rebellion that gives worship to the devil. Let's remember, God created mankind with the intent of their possessing His image and likeness alone!

> *And God said, Let us make man in our image, after our likeness: and let them have dominion over the fish of the sea, and over the fowl of the air, and over the cattle, and over all the earth, and over every creeping thing that creepeth upon the earth* (Genesis 1:26).

Although we were originally made after His spiritual image, when Adam fell, we lost His image and only retained His likeness (or bodily forms and emotional attributes). Since then, God has been seeking to restore His image to a dying world.

> *But we all, with open face beholding as in a glass the glory of the Lord, are changed into the same image from glory to glory, even as by the Spirit of the Lord* (2 Corinthians 3:18).

The devil also has an image, a fallen image. If we choose to be conformed to that image, then it is him we worship. Unfortunately, there is a grave price for this.

> *And the third angel followed them, saying with a loud voice, If any man worship the beast and his image, and receive his mark in his forehead, or in his hand, The same shall drink of the wine of the wrath of God, which is poured out without mixture into the cup of his indignation; and he shall be tormented with fire and brimstone in the presence of the holy angels, and in the presence of the Lamb: And the smoke of their torment ascendeth up for ever and ever: and they have no rest day nor night, who worship the beast and his image, and whosoever receiveth the mark of his name*
> (Revelation 14:9-11).

Does that mean all non-Christians are Satanists or witches, or have actively sought the occult? No, but one actively worships the devil when he or she decides to live a life of sin and separation from God. Satan does not seek to torment those in hell, but rather his efforts are to drive mankind into sin here on earth, so that by living under his influence, mankind may die under God's wrath.

Is Hell a Real Place?

On the whole, it is easier to reinterpret difficult topics found in Scripture than to trust God on the Bible's authenticity. Unfortunately, both Christians and non-Christians alike dispute the reality of hell because, for some, hell does not conform to their image of a loving God who would never allow people to suffer. But hell is literal and not symbolic! Hell is a real place, just as heaven is a real place. I have heard people say hell is only a separation from God, void of any kind of fire. Others have said that hell only has symbolic meaning. Many say that when Jesus talked about hell, He was referring to a place outside the Temple where animals were sacrificed, as a metaphor for what hell is like. While some things Jesus said held symbolic meaning toward a greater truth, all things He spoke were rooted in truth. Jesus is the living Word of God, (John 1:14) and while on earth, He never lied to the Church. Further, we can trust that He never will.

Henceforth I call you not servants; for the servant knows not what his lord does: but I have called you friends; for all things that I have heard of my Father I have made known to you (John 15:15).

That by two immutable things, in which it was impossible for God to lie, we might have a strong consolation, who have fled for refuge to lay hold upon the hope set before us (Hebrews 6:18).

Instead of denying the reality of hell, we need to realize that understanding hell is the key to knowing the fullness of Who God is and His love toward us.

To some, the concept of a place of eternal torment may not seem logical, but even logic itself can be subject to those things we know. In order to reason by logic, there must be some premise from which to operate. But what happens when we, on our best day with our *own* logic, cannot develop an accurate premise to begin to explain hell? Before we attempt to discredit the reality of hell, let's take a look at what the prophet Isaiah had to say about a *small* portion of the nature of God.

> *For my thoughts are not your thoughts, neither are your ways my ways, saith the LORD. For as the heavens are higher than the earth, so are my ways higher than your ways, and my thoughts than your thoughts* (Isaiah 55:8-9).

As humans, we are fundamentally disadvantaged when it comes to completely understanding God's nature in its fullness. Is it any wonder we find it difficult to understand the depths of what hell is like? The scriptures declare:

> *But as it is written, Eye hath not seen, nor ear heard, neither have entered into the heart of man, the things which God hath prepared for them that love Him* (1 Corinthians 2:9).

If we can accept that we cannot grasp all the good things to come that God has prepared for us, is it too far-fetched to think that there are some not-so-good things to come that we also cannot grasp? Therein is the wisdom of God revealed.

Our greatest glimpses into the supernatural are provided by believers in the Bible whom God has graced with supernatural experiences firsthand. Some include John's vision of heaven in the Book of Revelation, Paul's translation to the third heaven (2 Corinthians 12:2), Isaiah's vision of the throne of God (Isaiah 6), Ezekiel's vision of cherubim by the river Chebar (Ezekiel 1), or even the 70 elders who sat and ate dinner with God (Exodus 24:9-11). I believe there are many people in the world today who have experienced mighty wonders of God; it's just that we have yet to hear their testimony.

Does this firsthand experience dictate that we must abandon the use of logic in order to gain a greater understanding of God? Of course not! The apostle Paul is one of the greatest and most logical writers to be found in the New Testament. That doesn't negate the fact that some people today, in a failed attempt to comprehend God's rationale for creating hell, have watered all the scriptural components down in order to arrive at a concept they can mentally and morally deal with. Others simply strive to explain hell away.

Challenge to the Scriptures

Because of what seemed to be a glaring contradiction among the Scriptures, a local outspoken cleric once challenged a crowd of people on the authenticity of the Bible in the middle of the Florida A&M campus. His calling Christianity to the carpet deeply challenged my beliefs that day and forever changed how I would approach the difficult matters of God I needed to understand. Although many who heard his sermon accepted his position that the Bible had to be in error, I decided to talk to God and see what *He* had to say about it. I knew enough about God to know that He wasn't a liar, and I wasn't about to walk away from God just because someone told me not to trust Him.

When I arrived home that evening, I opened my Bible and pointed to the apparent contradiction. "I know there is an answer, and I'm not going to mistrust You," I told the Lord, "so could You let me know what it is?" After my short prayer, a light went on in my head and God presented to me the cleric's error. Not only was the topic *not* a contradiction as he'd alleged, but the answer was so simple I almost missed it. I went back to the campus the next day and the minister was still gloating over his success of the previous night.

He had gathered another crowd and had presented his thesis and question again. Now fully equipped with God's answer, I was eager to challenge this scoffer of Christianity. I made my way to the front and first stated the importance of utterly trusting in Christ and His Word. Then I answered his hard question. The answer silenced the cleric and stirred the people with an excitement that the Bible could be trusted. What a thrill when we trust in Christ, even when it doesn't make sense to do so!

I understood then, that there are many concepts in the Bible we may not yet understand, but that doesn't mean there is *no* understanding. We have to trust Christ and be willing to take time to pray and ask God for answers. As Ronald Kimble, the pastor of The Life Center in Orlando, Florida once said, "The difference between what we know and what we don't know is prayer and consecration!" We must allow those thoughts He describes as being "higher than our thoughts" (Isaiah 55:8) to pass through heaven's gates, float down to earth, and be deposited into our spirit.

God Still Reveals His Truths Today!

The scriptures declare that in the last days:

> *And it shall come to pass afterward, that I will pour out my spirit upon all flesh; and your sons and your daughters shall prophesy, your old men shall dream dreams, your young men shall see visions* (Joel 2:28).

God is still providing opportunities to peer into His glory, just as He did in the days of old. Hebrews 13:8 says: *Jesus Christ is the same yesterday, and today, and forever.*

The vision I received was unique because, unlike many people who describe life-after-death visitations to the other side, I had not died, as far as I know, nor had I been through a traumatic event beforehand. I'd been simply caught up in the spirit to this place. Paul described it best when he said:

> *It is not expedient for me doubtless to glory. I will come to visions and revelations of the Lord.*
> *I knew a man in Christ above fourteen years ago, (whether in the body, I cannot tell; or whether out of the body, I cannot tell: God knoweth); such a one caught up to the third heaven.*

> *And I knew such a man, (whether in the body, or out of the body,*
> *I cannot tell: God knoweth;)*
> *How that he was caught up into paradise, and heard*
> *unspeakable words, which it is not lawful for a man to utter*
> (2 Corinthians 12:1-4).

Although I do not fully understand the mechanics of how I was allowed to see and experience what I did, what took place after my arrival in hell is undeniable. My vision involved many types of woes. In order to relay this journey in a way for easier understanding, I will categorize hell's sufferings into three great torments: *the fire of hell, the memory of man, and the sense of utter hopelessness.* Each torment was no less devastating than the next, but together they comprise the essence of hell's savagery on the soul.

Yes, God supernaturally translated my soul to a place where I could not travel to on my own. This is the place I will attempt to tell you about.

Chapter 3

The Sea of Souls

Prompted by the combination of the pain and terror of my own experience, I, too, joined the wailing choir of the condemned.

The account I am about to relay to you happened in the fall of 1995. I had just arrived back at my apartment from a class at Florida A&M University and my mind was set on completing some chores before the day was through. But, when I unlocked my door and stepped past the doorframe, I was suddenly engulfed with the feeling of complete exhaustion and felt compelled to go and lie down. I was so purged of strength, I was certain I would collapse and fall asleep on the spot. It was as if I was wading through the basin of a pounding waterfall and the pressure of the deluge was pushing me level to the ground. Although I gave no special consideration to the strangeness of this experience, I instinctively staggered to my room where I surrendered to the overwhelming feeling of exhaustion and fell flat upon my bed.

The next moment I was *there*. The contrast was as different as if I'd been jerked from lounging before the crackle of a soothing fire, wrapped within the warmth of a soft comforter, to being plunged naked into ice-filled arctic waters. I went from the expectation of peaceful rest, to the horrible assault of sight, sound, mind, and soul.

The Noise of Hell

The instant I entered that place, immediately my hearing was bombarded with the explosive noise of the screaming of millions of people. The screaming assailed me from every direction, ferocious outcries of sufferings and unbearable anguish. That place was filled with what sounded like the wails of a multitude of worlds shrieking at once. Great choruses of torment reverberated endlessly in the air. The sound never lessened nor ceased, but instead, like ocean waves, continued furiously and relentlessly, washing over my ears as a physical bombardment. The incoming shrieks of the newly condemned steadily took up the screaming, while the souls who had been there only moments before had already lost their ability to scream.

My whole body changed from tangible flesh and blood to something intangible. My feet, legs, chest, and arms became translucent. I could literally see through myself.

You see, our human bodies originate from simple cells, which form an embryo, which divides and shapes itself to conform to our spiritual likeness. As such, our natural hair and teeth are only physical representatives of our spiritual bodies. King David said:

> *Thine eyes did see my substance, yet being unperfect; and in thy book all my members were written, which in continuance were fashioned, when as yet there was none of them* (Psalm 139:16).

Jesus' body shape and likeness were described in the scriptures long before His cells divided in Mary's womb to produce the physical likeness fashioned from His spiritual blueprint.

For he shall grow up before Him as a tender plant, and as a root out of a dry ground: he hath no form nor comeliness; and when we shall see Him, there is no beauty that we should desire Him
(Isaiah 53:2).

God's Spirit drives the duplication of cells, and there exists a spiritual pattern first before the earthly product becomes manifest. God said to Jeremiah:

Before I formed thee in the belly I knew thee; and before thou camest forth out of the womb I sanctified thee, and I ordained thee a prophet unto the nations (Jeremiah 1:5).

The Bible further shows that before men were created, angels were present at the creation of the earth, and thus predated man.

Where were you when I laid the earth's foundation?
Tell me, if you understand.
Who marked off its dimensions? Surely you know!
Who stretched a measuring line across it?
On what were its footings set,
or who laid its cornerstone—
while the morning stars sang together
and all the angels shouted for joy? (Job 38:4-7, NIV).

Although men and angels are not spiritual counterparts, it still must be noted that many of earth's creatures share physical commonality with angelic creatures. Ezekiel describes the cherubim he saw by the River Chebar as such:

> *Their faces looked like this: Each of the four had the face of a man, and on the right side each had the face of a lion, and on the left the face of an ox; each also had the face of an eagle* (Ezekiel 1:10).

The cherubim are also described as having eyes and hands beneath their wings. Therefore, the pattern of the earthly lion, ox, eagle and even the face of man had already been created in heaven long before man was formed from the dust of the earth! Glory to God!

No Questions Allowed

Like an antenna, my soul supernaturally served as a receptor to my surroundings. I knew things intrinsically in a way that my natural mind should not have known them. While there in the spirit, I became completely aware and I knew I had become a living soul. A great amount of knowledge poured into me; however, I was not experiencing omniscience. I know this, because I have no recollection of knowing anything more than what I'm describing. I didn't know why the others where there, or what they had done. That information was not for me to know.

It is important to understand that in hell, the knowledge that is available there does not come from any lessons learned or by someone instructing you. In that place, as you direct your attention toward an object, or if you question something in your mind, instantly the answer shoots back at you. However, the flip side is you don't ask any questions in hell. You *know* what it is you're seeing, even if you've never known about or seen what you're looking at before. Just as it is with a person coming out of a bad dream only to realize s/he has awakened to a reality far worse, this new ability only served to cement the authenticity of my current state. It was like a man driving in his car, who, while plunging to his death off a cliff, suddenly glances over and discovers the cell phone he'd been looking for earlier. What value does finding it hold now, in this situation, at this time?

Is It Possible to See in Hell?

A well-intentioned and respected theologian once argued that there were no flames in hell because flames, as we know them, produce light. Therefore, if hell is described as outer darkness, yet is filled with flames, there would also be light in hell, which would be a contradiction. What the theologian said would seem logical—*if you had not been there*. I think many believers would agree that God is not confined to the dictates of our human logic.

Revelations About Outer Darkness

One of the principles I learned while in that place was that light, in the natural, is fueled by natural things. Equally, supernatural light is fueled by supernatural things. Light that is produced in the supernatural is not composed of chemical reactions, earthly energy, or any manifestations such as candles, moonlight, or sunlight. The light that one encounters after death comes from one source, the spirit realm. That light is the Light that emanates from God and His Son. It is spiritual in nature and illuminates wherever God's glory abides (Psalms 139:8-13). No other sources of light are needed, except His. John wrote the truth when he penned:

> *And there shall be no night there; and they need no candle, neither light of the sun; for the Lord God giveth them light: and they shall reign forever and ever* (Revelation 22:5).

In the beginning, before God created the stars and moon, He pronounced, *Let there be light*, and it was so (Genesis 1:3-4, 14-18). But that light was not light radiating from created things; it was the light emanating from the Creator. And that light is not merely light to help you see things, but rather it is alive, it is His presence, His substance. It's the kind of living light that, if its rays strike your flesh as it did Moses' when he went up to the mount of God, your face would shine from inside out. It's the Glory of God!

> *And the city had no need of the sun, neither of the moon, to shine in it: for the glory of God did lighten it, and the Lamb is the light thereof* (Revelation 21:23).

Hell is the very absence of light. There are no shadows, nor shade, and even the darkness is not like the color that backdrops the midnight sky. As I looked, I could see no illuminating light, not even a tiny residue of light. There was no sun, moon, or stars in that place.

Although I wear glasses and need them to see things at a distance, in that place I could see clearly wherever I looked without any aid of corrective lenses. Amazingly, unlike on earth, I saw no vibrant colors in that place. There were no reds, blues, greens, or any other colors to glamorize or embellish anything in hell. On the contrary, there was no color at all.

This was revealed as truth to me about the nature of light: In the natural, we see things by reflected light, meaning the sun reflects off an object and we see the colors that make up that object. But in hell there was no external light source.

Hell's darkness is the very absence of *God's living, illuminating light.* There simply is no light in hell. The "outer" part of outer darkness comes from the Greek words *exo* and *exoteros,* meaning "complete," "outside of" (as in outdoors) or "put forth." We are shut completely from God's presence and the light that emanates from Him. That is why hell is described as outer darkness, because you are forever shut outside of God and the light and life that emanates from Him.

Hell's Fields

I did not see the texture of the ground I was standing upon, not because I did not notice, but because, given what I was going through, I honestly had no desire to examine it. I did realize, however, that I was standing on some flat, soul-filled plain that had no high or low parts, but rather, the surface was absolutely even. This is one attribute of my encounter that later struck me as being so deeply God-like. In hell, there are no platforms or high rises, no places where one can elevate oneself. All of our attempts to build our own prideful towers of Babel on earth, no matter how successful we were, come crumbling down in hell. In the end, everyone is on the same level. Like death, hell is a great equalizer of men. Both the great and the small are now categorized as The Condemned. When Isaiah described Satan's fall from heaven, he accurately captured this theme and foretold man's reaction to Satan at the end of days.

But you are brought down to the grave,
to the depths of the pit.
Those who see you stare at you,
they ponder your fate:
"*Is this the man who shook the earth*
and made kingdoms tremble,
the man who made the world a desert,
who overthrew its cities
and would not let his captives go home?"
(Isaiah 14:15-17, NIV).

No matter how pompous or exalted Satan spins his image to humans on earth, in the end, the final rewards to all of God's enemies are the same.

The Sea of Souls

It looked as if I were in some great body of water whose outer edges formed the shape of what appeared to be an expansive pit. At first glance, one might think I stood up to my neck in what appeared to be water, but it was not water at all. I was standing in the midst of a sea of human souls! Imagine if you will, looking down upon a packed rock concert in progress. Then imagine that same crowd multiplied by tens of millions. Then, instead of them jumping and shouting in adulation to the music, imagine them screaming and flaying their arms from the suffering and torments of being burned alive.

There were what seemed to be millions upon millions of people in that place. I could see people, like waves, bobbing up and down in this sea of souls, the waves being created by the arms and heads of those convulsing in pain, rising above the human horizon. It was horrific to behold. Rolling waves of earth's deceased inhabitants were all burning together; each person reduced to nothing more than an ember ingredient in a massive, hellish stew.

Rising right above my right shoulder, I caught the most tragic image I had ever seen. I saw the face and upper torso of a man who had just peaked over the soulish horizon, with one arm reaching above his head, while his fingers, all contorted, as if from horrible spasms, curled with pain. His countenance was shocking to look upon, his face twisted with the strain of suffering, and his eyes sunken deep into their sockets. His ghoulish skin was stretched taut across his body, as if he were horribly emaciated, and his mouth hung wide in the middle of a scream, yet no sound came from him. Then, like an ocean whale leaning back into the water after coming up for air, this wretched man who exuded the look of one who knows he is beyond the hope of help, fell sideward, blending into the undulating mass of souls.

I knew I was in hell. How tragic to me, that the subject of hell, which I had previously reduced to nothing more than a theory to be debated, now, by this experience, made any argument about its non-existence absurd. There was no satisfying "Ah Ha!" as if to point a self-congratulating finger at proving someone else wrong. There was only my regret that I had not taken at face value the scriptures concerning the reality of hell and applied them to my life before now.

I didn't know whether I'd died while sleeping or not, but one thing was indisputable to me, HELL IS REAL! Prompted by the combination of the pain and terror of my own experience, I, too, joined the wailing choir of the condemned.

The People of Hell

Therefore Hell hath enlarged herself, and opened her mouth without measure: and their glory, and their multitude, and their pomp, and he that rejoiceth, shall descend into it
(Isaiah 5:14).

I was surrounded completely with the souls of those who had died, both male and female. I saw people from all ages and times and races. I knew some to be from the nineteenth century, from the Middle Ages, American Indians, Asians, Blacks, Whites, all races. All were brothers and sisters in this torment. These were not people arrayed with differing garments of many colors like you might see walking down the street. Appearing with straw-like transparency and grayish in color, these people were souls without fleshy bodies. Like ghosts, these disembodied spirits were completely translucent but retained their forms and appearances, just as they did on earth. If you have ever taken a photograph and looked at its negative image, then that is close to what these souls looked like—everything clearly defined, including hands, feet, arms, size, and even shape. Many whom I saw wore clothes that made it easy to distinguish the origin of their time, but not all were fully garbed. Others, like an Indian man I saw, wore what I would consider to be traditional Native American attire.

In that place there was no concept of personal space. The souls were so close together it gave the impression of a blended mass of souls moving almost rhythmically together in pain. In that place no one could bump into another, and no one could take up another's space. People's shoulders seemed to merge in and out of other shoulders, bodies with other bodies. The nature of being a living soul removed the confinement and the solid boundaries of living inside flesh. In a natural body, we can bump into one another, and we can occupy space. Being surrounded by too many people can also crowd us. But in this place, no space was personal. If you moved to the left or right, you might just move inside the soul of another. The only posture I ever saw the souls take was an upright and standing one. I suspect that without the limitations of a physical body, they were free to stand forever.

I realized we retained our individual uniqueness in that place. We don't fade into nothingness or join the big light and lose our individuality, as some would suppose. We keep our identity, and in death we are able to think and process thoughts, even more clearly than in life. Proof of this can be found in 2 Samuel 28:15. When Samuel died, it was he who came back to *question King Saul*. When Moses and Elijah died (Matthew 17:1-13), it was they who returned to speak alone with Jesus on the Mount of Transfiguration and *gave Him instructions*.

In both cases, those who saw them instantly recognized them as the people they looked like when they were alive. Likewise, when we die, we are not dipped into nothingness and lose all forms of identity or thought, but rather, like in the moment when we were created, we became something unique that will forever retain its qualities. Yes, there were people from all times and ages standing around me, but I did not care to examine them, and neither did they stop to examine me, because we were all burning in flames!

Chapter 4

The First Great Torment: Fire

Upon entering the pit, instantaneously my senses exploded with pain. Out of the sheer impact of the fire upon my soul, my head arched back and I felt my eyes roll up in my head as I began to scream. It was like every fiber of my being produced a scream that struggled to explode from the depths of me, like a moth bursting from its cocoon. Louder and louder, the pitch of my scream increased without pause or breath. Like a voice moving from bass to tenor, climbing from alto to a screeching soprano, my voice climbed with pitch until the height of my scream could no longer mirror the depth of my suffering. It came from deep within me, bellowing up and out of me until my mouth was fully locked open, newly mute, in a horrific visage of pain.

The Weeping and Gnashing of Teeth

Why did my voice suddenly die? Have you ever realized that your vocal screams are relative to the pain you're subjected to? If you stub your toe, for instance, you might grunt. If you break a finger you might cry. If your limb is severed, you might scream. We respond depending upon the level of pain we are subjected to.

There comes a point, however, when the sound we make cannot match the pain that we feel. In hell, when you come to that point, the sound coming from your mouth ceases. What happens next? The scriptures adequately portray the reality. As if to stretch your jaw wide to relieve it from some horrible cramping, in hell all you can do is open and close your mouth violently, clashing your teeth together again and again soundlessly. Thus, Jesus' prophecy in Matthew 22:13 is fulfilled: *There will be a weeping and gnashing of teeth.*

I had always wanted to understand what Jesus meant when He spoke this scripture, and now I had became an unwilling student of suffering's truths.

The Pain

I don't remember seeing anyone running or shifting positions to get to another location. All were too caught up in the agony that made them scream to even care about moving. The United States military has experimented with tactical warfare techniques, such as sensory overload, before engaging targets that may be armed and dangerous. They have employed weapons, like flash bangs, that serve to distract the target. When assaulting a location, troops would subject the enemy's natural senses to either extreme light or noise, which in effect paralyzes them long enough for the assault to be successful. Now, utilizing that same principle, try to imagine the *spiritual* senses being overloaded by such intense pain that moving is not an option.

The closest thing to movement in that place is the convulsing that's produced by intense waves of pain. Even with all the violent seizures of those burning, no one can be struck by another. As a participant in this torment, another truth was revealed to me. The capability to inflict pain or damage on another was impossible because bodies are in an intangible state. Consequently, should you end up there, like a great stroke from the blade of God's justice, all the pain in that place is felt by you and you alone forever. No one else can be hurt by you ever again.

The Breath of Hell

And in Hell he lifted up his eyes, being in torments . . .
(Luke 16:23).

People will lift up their eyes in hell. You cannot help it. The lifting of my eyes was my soul's natural reaction to being swallowed in such an unforgiving inferno. I was completely absorbed with fire. Truly, I understand why the flames in Luke 16:23 were described as torments, because it was as if the ground itself was exploding with fire. Like frantic breathing emanating from the lungs, the ground exhaled fire on me and then inhaled it back within itself, with less than instants between each torturous breath. Neverending waves of fire roared up and down my body, producing such an unearthly pain that I cannot adequately express the awful sensation with words. After being touched by this hellish flame initially, my soul became like an inflamed pain receptor, with no momentary relief between the breaths of fire. Never in life had I even come close to imagining this, let alone experiencing such pain. The fire was everywhere, and everyone in that place was burning.

In the natural, by igniting wood, clothing, or some other object, fire is perpetuated. But neither I nor anyone else assisted the flame by providing a fuel source, because the fire was self-burning, self-perpetuating. It roared up through my soul as if I were in its way. My body was replete with this ferocious flame, yet it was not kindled upon me. If my flesh were present to burn, it would have been a sweet cushion before this flame hit my soul.

Even in tragic burn cases, the pain sensors of the victims are destroyed by fire before the body is consumed. In hell, there is no deadening of pain sensors that the burning of the flesh allows you. As I experienced it, there was nowhere to move, or any way to shake the fire off. It was relentless. I couldn't extinguish it by patting out the flames, because I had no solid surfaces to pat. This flame could not be fanned away, because it came from the ground itself. Nothing you could try would matter. The flames ravaged my soul mercilessly and I was completely powerless against its onslaught. It roared up through my feet, inside my chest, and out the top of my head. There was no one to help me, and I had no recourse but to burn. Oh, what a wretched soul I had become!

The Barrier Between Life and Death

Once, I imagined hell as a deep chasm, with jagged, descending walls and fire emanating out of its mouth. After appearing in that place, I saw there were no mountain walls to speak of, or walls of any kind you could see, but there was a barrier as solid as it was impassable, and it separated my soul from the land of the living. It was horrible! I wanted to leave but there was nowhere to go. I knew I could not cross back into the land of the living, neither had I any means to do so. I recall thinking, *just one second prior I was in the land of the living, yet now I am here lifting my eyes up in hell.*

Out of the multitude of terrible things that went through my mind, I remembered one distinct and personal thought. I remarked to myself, *I would rather live an eternity having my head crushed under the wheel of a truck on the other side of this barrier, in the land of the living, than to spend another moment in hell.* Oh, how sweet a thought like that seemed at the time! It was at this very moment I realized that I could not shed a tear. I knew tears were a natural occurrence to expel strong, negative or positive emotions, and can, at the very least, be therapeutic. But, the weeping in that place was not aided by the release of tears. There is no liquid to expel from the spiritual body.

The weeping exceeded all weeping I have ever known or seen. I have watched documentaries of the women of war-ravaged territories, weeping over their lost loved ones. But no amount of lost men, women, or children can prepare you for the weeping produced by hell. The weeping of hell's residents rang out as a dry, repressive, and futile outcry in which the sweet release of liquid tears did not come.

What the Flames Looked Like

For a couple of years after my experience, I struggled to find an adequate analogy to describe what this fire looked like. My answer came from an unexpected source. One Saturday afternoon, I turned to a sports broadcast that was reporting the facts from a recent car accident. As I watched the sports footage, a man, running frantically, acted as if he were burning from some unseen force, but I could see no flames. One journalist described the incident like this:

"Robby Gordon lasted just three laps on the restart of the Indianapolis 500 today before his car caught on fire, burning his right leg and hand. Gordon was fourth when the green flag dropped on lap 18 after two warm-up laps under yellow, and he appeared to be moving up when all of a sudden he drove onto the pit road in turn three. Gordon quickly parked the car, flung his steering wheel out and ran away while a methanol fire burned his right leg and hand. In a few tortuous seconds before a safety worker arrived with a fire extinguisher, Gordon rolled around in the grass trying to put out the invisible blaze."[3]

You see, certain racecars use a fuel called methanol to propel high-powered engines. Methane gas is described as colorless, odorless gas (at room temperature).[4] Bacterial decomposition in *landfills* also produces methane, which can be harnessed as an energy source. Sea worms have also been found on the floor of the Gulf of Mexico that lives on *methane hydrates.*

When a methanol fire breaks out in one of these cars, the fire burns invisibly, except for the accompanying heat wave.[5] In this case, no one could tell what was wrong with the driver until he came up close, and then the visual distortions of heat could be seen in the air. Robby Gordon's crew realized he was on fire. Methanol fire is fire, but it burns clear!

Hell's Pure Fire

Many times I've heard stories of people who return from the dead and describe a light they saw at the end of a tunnel. After emerging from the end of that tunnel, they often meet their loved ones who had passed on, or they even meet Jesus Himself. The common thread running through all these stories is that the light they encountered was not like the normal light we have on earth. It's brighter and purer. I have heard it described as being so brilliant that the normal sun and stars look dark compared to it. This radiance resembled light, but it was more than light.

As I've stated before, this light was true *Light*. It was the original after which all others are patterned. Just as that Light cannot be compared to common earthly light, I learned also that the fire that sets hell aflame is nothing like the kind of flame most of us are familiar with, yet its still fire. Hell's flames did not dance with the colors of amber, orange, or even blue-green tendrils. It was clear! It was pure fire; there were no distortions of heat waves, no smoke, and no colors. It erupted up and through the body with no indication of ceasing, yet remained as untraceable as the wind in its goings and comings. No proof of one's torment was evident except the painful blight left on the soul.

Chapter 5

The Second Great Torment: The Memory of Man

> *. . . And shall cut him asunder, and appoint him his portion with the hypocrites: there shall be weeping and gnashing of teeth* (Matthew 24:51).

Thoughts of a Condemned Soul

I learned a valuable lesson about the judgment of the soul in that place. I always visualized the judgment of a human soul in terms of dying, standing before the throne of God, and in some way pleading your case as to why you should go to heaven for the good things you have done rather than go to hell for the bad things. The scene I'd imagined was akin to having my day in court to explain my side of the story.

I quickly found out that I was in error. My first mistake was to believe that at any point in my life God ever took his eyes off me. And because He never took his eyes off me, no opportunity was needed to explain any situation He already knew about in absolute detail.

In a moment shall they die, and the people shall be troubled at midnight, and pass away: and the mighty shall be taken away without hand. For His eyes are upon the ways of man, and he seeth all his goings. There is no darkness, nor shadow of death, where the workers of iniquity may hide themselves. For he will not lay upon man more than right; that he should enter into judgment with God (Job 34:20-23).

God is omniscient and He knows all things. God is the ultimate witness regarding anyone's soul. He knows what I did, how I did it, where I did it, and what my intent was. He knows when I did it, and His testimony is indisputable! So then, as the scriptures declare:

It is appointed unto men once to die, and after that the judgment (Hebrews 9:27).

I understood that the end of my life was not the beginning of judgment, but rather, the slamming of the gavel. Death marked the moment where court has been adjourned concerning my life and the verdict and sentence are now sealed. God had done all He could to prevent disaster, and what I was now going to face was the result of my own will.

For there is nothing hid, which shall not be manifested; neither was any thing kept secret, but that it should come abroad
(Mark 4:22).

God had done all the things He could for me to choose right and yet I did not. Now, after my death, there was no more holding back from God, no more chances, no more calls to repentance. I realized that my whole life God had been watching, and now that I'd died, the judgment I received was the result of every choice I'd made in my life, whether good or bad. In hell I realized I was about to eat the fruit of the life I had sown.

There was no break in the proceedings. My last action would be the exclamation point on the life I had lived. Now death was just the bailiff that ushered me to my reward, either to eternal freedom or to eternal punishment. In this case, it was punishment. The judgment was instantaneous and without question, and oddly enough, I agreed with the verdict. I knew my judgment was the direct result of the wrongs I had committed while in the land of the living, for my own conscience served as the prosecution's witness.

> *For when the Gentiles, which have not the law, do by nature the things contained in the law, these, having not the law, are a law unto themselves: Which shew the work of the law written in their hearts, their conscience also bearing witness, and their thoughts the mean while accusing or else excusing one another; In the day when God shall judge the secrets of men by Jesus Christ according to my gospel* (Romans 2:14-16).

Shortly after I began to write this book, I asked a friend what comes to his mind whenever he thinks of hell. His reply brought to my attention a fact that had escaped my awareness because, as a former resident of hell, I considered the truth blatantly obvious. He said, "When I think of hell, I see a place full of confusion and disorientation." After a moment or two of pensive thought, I looked at him and stated, "Hell is the last place you'll be confused!"

> *Confusion: bewilderment, the act of confusing somebody or something, or the state of being confused or perplexed. Or, lack of clarity; misunderstanding of a situation or the facts thereof.*[6]

My friend's response brought to light the degree to which one is fully aware of his own actions in that place. I went on to explain, "There is no confusion or surprise in hell." As a matter of fact, you are more lucid and aware than you had been in life. There is no surprise regarding why you are there. What's even more intriguing, you completely agree that you *should* be there. There is no misunderstanding that the road you chose to travel led you to wind up at this spiritual dead end.

As if a veil over my mind had been snatched away, all my memories came into focus in absolute, crisp detail. Many people have described how, in a moment of great peril, their whole life passed before their eyes. Images of significant moments, good and bad, are replayed instantly. You are able to draw on every piece of information that was available to you during your lifetime because it is all a part of your soul's memory, not your mind's. What the mind can forget, the soul cannot! The mind is the place where the memories are replayed, but the soul is the place where the memories reside.

The Soul's Role in Memory Retention

For what man knoweth the things of a man, save the spirit of man which is in him? even so the things of God knoweth no man, but the Spirit of God (1 Corinthians 2:11).

This truth came alive to me in an instant: Your spirit/soul records every action or experience you have ever gone through. This is what the world calls the subconscious mind. Your soul then transfers that information to your physical brain, through chemical and electrical processes, and only then can you remember. Once that information is stored into your physical brain, it becomes part of the conscious mind. But the conscious mind is not capable of knowing any more than what is collected in the soul. That's why before a person is born again through faith in Jesus Christ, he can *only* perceive those things his soul learned from the natural world. This information is transferred as information to his natural mind.

When a person is born again in Christ Jesus, the arena in which his spirit draws information now comes from both the natural and spiritual worlds, hence *so the things of God knoweth no man, save [by] the Spirit [or Holy Spirit] of God.*

The transfer of information to the conscious mind is the same in both the saved and unsaved person. The main difference is that when a soul is born again, that soul is changed into a *new creature* (2 Corinthians 5:17), which is now a spiritual receptor for spiritual things, as well as for natural ones.

So, when God speaks to our spirits, that information is first processed by the spirit and then transferred to our natural minds. For example, when Christians speak in tongues, the information relayed in that heavenly prayer is first received within a believer's spirit, and out of their spirit they utter angelic words. But the mind, (conscious mind), does not comprehend.

> *For if I pray in an unknown tongue, my spirit prayeth, but my understanding is unfruitful* (1 Corinthians 14:14).

Our understanding is unfruitful because that information is not transferred to our conscious minds. Before the information our spirit is receiving and praying about can be transferred to our conscious mind, Paul instructs us to pray for interpretation in 1 Corinthians 14:13: *Wherefore let him that speaketh in an unknown tongue pray that he may interpret* (or bring that knowledge into his conscious mind).

The process of all cognitive thought does not begin in our fleshly brains, but rather from within the soul of man. That is why when the fleshly brain is damaged, it can no longer process information, like a computer struck by lightning. But if that brain is allowed to heal, then it can again start processing more information from the spirit to the mind. When you study, the information is stored in your soul, or subconscious mind, but it must then be withdrawn and deposited into the conscious mind, or natural brain, in order to be of use.

Even Jesus said of the Holy Spirit:

> *But the Helper, the Holy Spirit, whom the Father will send in My name, He will teach you all things, and bring to your remembrance all that I said to you* (John 14:26).

So, in order to bring it back, we must first put it in!

This brings me to a unique thought about the physiology of the human body. Science, through certain techniques, can help people recall memories of things they have *consciously* forgotten. But the subconscious mind does not forget. It retains all memory of everything we have ever seen or experienced in our lives. With a purpose in mind, God gave us everything we have.

Imagine a world where we cannot forget our own mistakes or the wrongs done by others. What if we lived in a world where we could not eliminate the images of horror or tragedy, but instead they replayed in the forefront of our minds every waking hour?

In 1993, I worked for a short time in Washington D.C. at the White House in the Office of Agency Liaison, under the Clinton Administration. While there, I was privy to many letters written by America's veterans who were experiencing post-traumatic stress syndrome. After reading numerous such letters, I realized that there are many former soldiers who wish they could forget certain horrific wartime images.

Here is where the wisdom of God is revealed. The purpose of the conscious mind is not only to remember, but also to forget! By the simple act of forgetting, we are released from some of life's worst experiences.

The reality of the subconscious, or soul, is that it cannot forget. Like a sculptor's knife etching a piece of soft clay, every memory is recorded and those memories shape the type of person you are. When you are a disembodied spirit, you cannot hide behind the forgetfulness of the conscious mind. Your soul is an eternal recorder that cannot lie to itself, nor convince itself of any thing other than the truth. To a person who lives a life without God, his own soul is his most honest and worst enemy.

In the soul all actions are recorded and replayed. While burning in hell, my mind replayed every opportunity given to me to change or repent. My mind remembered clearly every Christian radio program I'd heard, whether in my own car, or passing someone else's who had his or her window down. I remembered every tract on the ground that I had ever stepped over that pricked my mind to repent from a sin or change a lifestyle or habit. I remembered every sermon preached, and every television program that ever encouraged me to yield my heart back to God or to love my neighbor. I remembered everything I had ever done. I knew every opportunity ever given to me to repent, change, or to be kind.

It is because of this replay of the choices I'd made during my lifetime that I could understand the justice of my condemnation. I knew that I was not just guilty, but *deserving* of what I was suffering.

This fact brings out something intriguing about the story of the rich man who went to hell (Luke 16:19-31). In his request to Abraham, the rich man never asked to be freed, but rather asked for Lazarus to go back to his brothers and warn them. Why didn't he ask for pardon? Instead of asking Abraham to send some water, why did he not ask to send some angels to get *him* out of there? Why, during everything he said, was there no hint of a request to free him from his sentence, but rather an expression of a sincere desire to stop others from coming there? The reason is clear. He knew he'd *chosen* to ignore the message of Moses and the prophets on earth and now he was resigned to reap the rewards of his self-centered life in hell.

Chapter 6

The Third Great Torment: The Sense of Utter Hopelessness

The nature of hope is a strange thing, and it takes on many different forms. Some people lose their minds as a way of either coping or being freed from the pain or trauma of their experiences. In this, they find a *kind* of reprieve from all the suffering they are going through, albeit, a shallow reprieve. But there is no *hope* of insanity in hell. There is no hope at all, either in things good or things bad. All hope is gone. One would think hope for insanity is a bad thing, but in that place it would still be hope. There is no frailty of the flesh there. There is no mental illness in hell; you are who you are in hell, and you experience what you experience in the purest sense.

The result of this understanding is a deep emotion of regret that is as fathomless as a bottomless sea. Utter hopelessness is the hardest of my hellish experiences to describe because the feeling of loss my soul experienced defies description.

Knowing what you were supposed to do and yet having the knowledge that you will never have another opportunity to do anything more about the thing you've left undone or done wrong is heartrending. Knowing God's judgment is righteous and absolutely flawless and just concerning every aspect of your life is what spawns this complete and utter sense of hopelessness. Gabriele Amorth, chief exorcist of Rome, wrote in his book, *An Exorcist Tells His Story*, about an encounter with a devil:

"One day Father Candido asked a [possessed] thirteen-year-old girl, "Two enemies, who hated each other all their lives, hated each other to death, and both ended up in Hell. What is the relationship that they will share now, since they will be with each other for all eternity?" And this was the Devil's response: "How stupid you are! Down there everyone lives folded within himself and torn apart by his regrets. There is no relationship with anyone; everyone finds himself in the most profound solitude and desperately weeps for the evil that he has committed."[7]

Hell would be easier to cope with if one was able to claim false imprisonment in some form of unrighteous indignation, because if that were the case, you could feel victimized by your situation and have a reason to hate, be angry, or feel mistreated. But in hell you understand the horrible choices you've made, and all your hope is lost. The scriptures were prophetically accurate when in Ecclesiastes 9:4 King Solomon states: *For to him that is joined to all the living there is hope: for a living dog is better than a dead lion.* In hell you are outside of any chance of changing your ways or your situation. I knew that the greatest thing I'd possessed on earth was God, and now God was gone from me.

You realize you will never be bathed or clothed in God's presence again. Have you ever closed your eyes, yet knew someone stood close to you, so close you could almost feel their presence like a force? That's how the feeling of God's presence is. God's presence is in everything; all created things are held together by it.

One God and Father of all, who is above all, and through all, and in you all (Ephesians 4:6).

For by Him were all things created, that are in heaven, and that are in earth, visible and invisible, whether they be thrones, or dominions, or principalities, or powers: all things were created by Him, and for Him: And he is before all things, and by Him all things consist (Colossians 1:16,17).

Now imagine the absence of this presence. In hell you know beyond a shadow of doubt that *all good and perfect things come from Him* (James 1:17), and now you know that the source of all those things will forever elude you. We as humans cannot fully comprehend the abundance of God's presence in the earth. It is what gives the trees, grass, and earth its life and beauty. Though all have experienced His presence, we oftentimes deny it. It is like someone who never took notice of the beauty of breathing until an asthma attack strips that privilege away. Suddenly she realizes that air is the most precious thing in her life, and yet, now it's gone. You will never realize that God is all that matters, until nothing else matters.

Tragically, I now came to truly appreciate and acknowledge His abiding presence in my life, only because it was gone. I saw how I had squandered both my time on earth and my opportunities to experience His presence, and I was swallowed up with tremendous sorrow. All was lost and there was no hope for me anymore. While my mouth tried to scream, my heart was hollow, overwhelmed with the loss of my own soul forever separated from its Creator.

Over But Not Finished

It was then that I returned abruptly to the reality of my bedroom, speechless from the vision. I rolled over from my prostrate position and sat up on the edge of my bed. Stunned beyond measure by what I'd just seen and experienced, I cried out in pity for myself that I'd been chosen to bear witness to what hell was like. That may seem selfish, but I cried for myself because I had not asked to see this vision, and yet it had been shown to me.

> *The more you know, the more you hurt; the more you understand, the more you suffer* (Ecclesiastes 1:18, CEV).

I sat on my bed shaking from the images of millions of people burning. I fell on my knees and prayed, "Jesus, keep me from this place!" I wept for those souls that were generational residents of such horrors. There were so many souls in hell that I could do nothing for! I wept because I know many people living on earth today do not know what I had just learned, and are bound to become part of the choir of the condemned. I wept because so many seconds in my day are spent frivolously, without my notice, and yet, for the souls I burned with, the flames demanded every second of their attention. I wept because I understood that God *is* truly a loving and just God and what I witnessed did not have to happen to anyone else if they would repent from sin and believe on Jesus Christ to save them from this fate. I wept because I knew that my life would never be the same.

Chapter 7

Common Mistakes and Misunderstandings About Hell

Oftentimes, our beliefs about commonly quoted or under taught passages can be in error if we do not properly identify the assumptions made concerning these scriptures. Following are three frequently misunderstood concepts.

Misunderstanding #1: ***AND THE GATES OF HELL SHALL NOT PREVAIL AGAINST THE CHURCH*** REFERS TO THE ARMIES OF SATAN, WHICH SHALL NOT PREVAIL OVER THE CHURCH.

One of the most widely used scripture that is often misunderstood is:

> *When Jesus came into the coasts of Caesarea Philippi, he asked his disciples, saying, Whom do men say that I the Son of man am? And they said, Some say that thou art John the Baptist: some, Elias; and others, Jeremias, or one of the prophets. He saith unto them, But whom say ye that I am? And Simon Peter answered and said, Thou art the Christ, the Son of the living God.*
> *And Jesus answered and said unto him, Blessed art thou, Simon Barjona: for flesh and blood hath not revealed it unto thee, but my Father which is in heaven. And I say also unto thee, That thou art Peter, and upon this rock I will build my church; and the gates of Hell shall not prevail against it* (Matthew 16:13-18).

Many well-meaning Christians have used these words of scripture as proof that Satan has a kingdom of demons moving back and forth from hell, assaulting the Christian body. While this imagery does much to prepare the Christian mind for spiritual warfare, when we quote this scripture out of context, we miss the real truth and power found in this verse, and may overlook other scriptures that better prepare us for warfare. To understand the power and meaning behind this passage we must first comply with Paul's instruction on interpreting Scripture:

> *Study to shew thyself approved unto God, a workman that needeth not to be ashamed, rightly dividing the Word of truth* (2 Timothy 2:15).

An innocent mistake of misinterpretation of Scripture can cause basic errors in our thinking about the enemy. This can lead to gaping holes in our spiritual defenses. Matthew 16:13-18 reveals God's plan of salvation to the world.

> *When Jesus came into the coasts of Caesarea Philippi, he asked his disciples, saying, Whom do men say that I the Son of man am? And they said, Some say that thou art John the Baptist: some, Elias; and others, Jeremias, or one of the prophets. He saith unto them, But whom say ye that I am?* (Matthew 16:13-18).

Point: In this verse, Jesus asked Peter to respond to a question: *Whom say ye that I am?* In Peter's case, his response reflected the Holy Spirit's work to bring an inward revelation into his heart that Jesus *is Lord*. That is just one of the roles the Holy Spirit plays in the initiating work of salvation for unbelievers. *Inward belief* is the *root* of every unbeliever's confession.

> *And Simon Peter answered and said; Thou art the Christ, the Son of the living God.*

Point: Once the Holy Spirit has made known to the unbeliever exactly who Jesus Christ is, confession that Jesus is Lord follows. So, *outward confession* is the *fruit* of the inward belief that Jesus Christ is Lord.

And Jesus answered and said unto him, Blessed art thou,
Simon Barjona: for flesh and blood hath not revealed it unto
thee,
but my Father which is in heaven.

Point: Jesus told Peter that his confession had been prompted by the will of the Father, through the means of the Holy Spirit, which resulted in Peter's acknowledgment of Who Christ is, and the position He now held in Peter's life. Literally, Peter followed the pattern later termed "the plan of salvation." Glory to God!

> *That if thou shalt confess with thy mouth* [fruit] *the Lord Jesus, and shalt believe in thine heart* [root] *that God hath raised Him from the dead, thou shalt be saved. For with the heart man believeth unto righteousness* [root]; *and with the mouth confession is made unto salvation* [fruit] (Romans 10:9-10).

Point: Jesus goes on to establish confession through the work of the Holy Spirit by the will of the Father as a principle that will cause the Church to be established. As Jesus said:

> *And I say also unto thee, that thou art Peter, and upon this rock I will build my church; and the gates of Hell shall not prevail against it* (Matthew 16:18).

Point: The rock Jesus was referring to was not just a play on words because Peter's name means rock. But rather, Jesus' literal use of the word *rock* establishes the context that helps to understand this scripture. What is a rock, and how has Jesus used it in scriptures? A rock, in scriptural terms, means a foundation, on which all things are built.

> *Whosoever cometh to me, and heareth my sayings, and doeth them, I will shew you to whom he is like: He is like a man which built an house, and digged deep, and laid the foundation on a rock:*

*and when the flood arose, the stream beat vehemently upon
that house, and could not shake it: for it was founded upon a
rock. But he that heareth, and doeth not, is like a man that
without a foundation built an house upon the earth; against
which
the stream did beat vehemently, and immediately it fell;
and the ruin of that house was great*
(Luke 6:47-49).

Point: Upon the faith-filled confession that Jesus is the Christ, Jesus proclaimed, *I will build my church*. In other words, the Church will not grow through special dinners or secular appeals, but rather through the preaching and confession of Christ. So, with Matthew 16:13-18 understood in this light, what did Jesus mean when he said, (*the gates of Hell shall not prevail against the church*?) Jesus was referring to the fact that *death* shall not prevail against the *confession that Jesus is the Christ*. The Church's confession that Jesus is Lord guarantees us that as believers we will be resurrected to eternal life by Him and Him alone. And when that happens, death will have no hold on us. Without Christ, resurrection from the dead into new life would not be possible.

*I am he that liveth, and was dead; and, behold, I am alive
for evermore, Amen; and have the keys of Hell and of death*
(Revelation 1:18).

Point: For what reason does Jesus hold these keys except to open gates, referring to Gates of Hell (that power which keeps men from resurrecting). Jesus unlocked the grave and death so that we could be resurrected in our own transformed bodies just as Christ's body was resurrected to eternal life. Up until this time, no one had been resurrected from the dead and *remained alive* for all of eternity, but Jesus was resurrected on the third day as a forerunner for you and me.

Misunderstanding #2: IN THE BIBLE, *HELL* MEANS THE SAME THING WHENEVER IT IS MENTIONED.

It is important to know that there are different Greek and Hebrew words used for hell. Where these words are used, none are referring to hell as a kingdom of Satan, nor are they referring to an attack of the enemy. These words are as follows:

A. (Greek) *Gehenna*: Name or place or state of everlasting punishment. This is the word Jesus used to describe the place of everlasting torment. This hell, or place of torment, the devil does not want to go to. It is a place originally prepared for the devil and his angels (Matthew 25:41), but also serves as a place of torment for those who reject God.

Scriptural Uses:

> *But I say unto you, That whosoever is angry with his brother without a cause shall be in danger of the judgment: and whosoever shall say to his brother, Raca, shall be in danger of the council: but whosoever shall say, Thou fool, shall be in danger of Hell [Gehenna] fire* (Matthew 5:22).

> *Ye serpents, ye generation of vipers, how can ye escape the damnation of Hell [Gehenna]?* (Matthew 23:33).

> *And if thine eye offend thee, pluck it out, and cast it from thee: it is better for thee to enter into life with one eye, rather*

than having two eyes to be cast into Hell [Gehenna] *fire*
(Matthew 18:9).

And fear not them which kill the body, but are not able to kill the soul: but rather fear Him which is able to destroy both soul and body in Hell [Gehenna] (Matthew 10:28).

But I will forewarn you whom ye shall fear: Fear Him, which after he hath killed hath power to cast into Hell [Gehenna]; yea, I say unto you, Fear Him (Luke 12:5).

B. (Greek) *Tartaros:* abyss, pit, to be incarcerated in hell. The word *pit*, as used in Revelation 9, means a hole in the ground meant for *holding* something, like a well or cistern, for example.

This is the word used for the bottomless pit of darkness that a certain number of the fallen angels are chained within, waiting to be unleashed in the last days of man. Notice, all these angels are chained in hell [Tartaros] and not roaming free.

Scriptural Uses:

> *For if God spared not the angels that sinned, but cast them down to Hell [Tartaros], and delivered them into chains of darkness, to be reserved unto judgment . . .* (2 Peter 2:4).

Point: These chained, fallen angels had a king over them, and this king was the fifth of seven angels who stand before God (Revelation 8:2) to blow the trumpets signaling the release of woes on earth (Revelation 9:1-2). This fifth angel named *Abaddon*, like the sixth angel (Revelation 9:13-14), was a heavenly angel who was given the power to release and bind the fallen angels.

> *And the fifth angel sounded, and I saw a star fall from heaven unto the earth: and to him [the fifth angel] was given the key of the bottomless pit. And he opened the bottomless pit; and there arose a smoke out of the pit, as the smoke of a great furnace; and the sun and the air were darkened by reason of the smoke of the pit* (Revelation 9:1-2).

> *And they had a king over them, which is the angel of the bottomless pit, whose name in the Hebrew tongue is Abaddon, but in the Greek tongue hath his name Apollyon* (Revelation 9:11).

> *And I saw an angel come down from heaven, having the key of the bottomless pit and a great chain in his hand* (Revelation 20:1-3).

And he laid hold on the dragon, that old serpent, which is the Devil, and Satan, and bound him a thousand years, And cast him into the bottomless pit, and shut him up, and set a seal upon him, that he should deceive the nations no more, till the thousand years should be fulfilled: and after that he must be loosed a little season (Revelation 20:2).

C. (Greek) *Hades*: Place of departed souls, grave, a place of disembodied souls. Christ was never sent to [Gehenna] Hell. The following scriptures refer to the grave [Hades].

Scriptural Uses:

> *And I say also unto thee, that thou art Peter, and upon this rock I will build my church; and the gates of Hell [Hades] shall not prevail against it* (Matthew 16:18).

> *Because thou wilt not leave my soul in Hell [Hades], neither wilt thou suffer thine Holy One to see corruption. Thou hast made known to me the ways of life; thou shalt make me full of joy with thy countenance. Men and brethren, let me freely speak unto you of the patriarch David, that he is both dead and buried, and his sepulchre is with us unto this day. Therefore being a prophet, and knowing that God had sworn with an oath to him, that of the fruit of his loins, according to the flesh, he would raise up Christ to sit on his throne; He seeing this before spake of the resurrection of Christ, that his soul was not left in Hell, neither his flesh did see corruption* (Acts 2:27-31).

Point: It is important to note that God stated he would not leave Jesus' soul in the grave [Hades] and thus see corruption (decay), but Jesus got up on the third day in fulfillment of Scripture! The Book of Acts validates this:

> *He seeing this before spake of the resurrection of Christ, that his soul was not left in Hell, neither his flesh did see corruption* (Acts 2:31).

D. (Hebrew) *Sheol*: the Old Testament Hebrew equivalent of the New Testament word *hades*. It means the world of the dead.

Scriptural Uses:

> *Whither shall I go from thy spirit? or whither shall I flee from thy presence? If I ascend up into heaven, thou art there: if I make my bed in Hell [Sheol], behold, thou art there* (Psalm 139:7-8).

Point: David used the word *Sheol* in his psalms to describe the presence of God in the life of God's people. Even if David were separated from his body (not condemned to suffering in the fires of Gehenna), God's presence would still be with him. We see this principle vividly in the scriptures. Sometimes, even in death, God's presence can be so mighty upon his chosen that miracles happen.

> *And Elisha died, and they buried him. And the bands of the Moabites invaded the land at the coming in of the year. And it came to pass, as they were burying a man, that, behold, they spied a band of men; and they cast the man into the sepulchre of Elisha: and when the man was let down, and touched the bones of Elisha, he revived, and stood up on his feet* (2 Kings 13:20-21).

Misunderstanding #3: THE LAKE OF FIRE IS THE SAME AS HELL.

The lake of fire is *not* the same as hell. The lake of fire is the final place of torment for both angels and men at the end of time. At that point, all men will be resurrected before God one last time, some to death, and some to eternal life.

> *. . . And shall come forth; they that have done good, unto the resurrection of life; and they that have done evil, unto the resurrection of damnation* (John 5:29).

Also . . .

> *I saw the dead, great and small; they stood before the throne, and books were opened. Then another book was opened, which is the Book of Life. And the dead were judged by what they had done in accordance with what was recorded in the books. And the sea delivered up the dead who were in it, death and Hades* (the state of death or disembodied existence) *surrendered the dead in them, and all were tried and their cases determined by what they had done. Then death and Hades were thrown into the lake of fire. This is the second death, the lake of fire. And if anyone's name was not found recorded in the Book of Life; he was hurled into the lake of fire* (Revelation 20:12-15).

Point: It is important to note that what I experienced was not a lake of fire as found in the Book of Revelation. Yes, fire flowed from that place where I was and the number of souls writhing there resembled an ocean, but the lake of fire is reserved for a different time and season. The lake is reserved for the end of time as we know it.

While sharing with a minister friend about the experience, he brought to my attention that I did not mention brimstone or smoke. But if smoke and brimstone are indeed in hell, I didn't have any recollection of the sulphur smell, or seeing brimstone. As I said, I was a participant and not just an observer, and only what I experienced and know can I relay here.

However, I went home to search the scriptures and study what I could about the places where smoke and brimstone are used. As I poured over all occurrences of brimstone in the scriptures, I came across two types. The first was the type God rained down from heaven in His wrath, i.e. on Sodom and Gomorrah (*Deuteronomy 29:23; Job 18:15; Psalm 11:6; Isaiah 30:33; Isaiah 34:9; Ezekiel 38:22; Luke 17:29; Revelation 9:17; Revelation 9:18*).

The context and use of the word brimstone, however, drastically changes starting in Revelation chapter 14, verse 10, and continuing throughout the rest of the book. From Revelation we learn that brimstone bellows up from the fiery tomb of all those that are in service to Satan. I discovered that brimstone is used in reference to the lake of fire, the place of final punishment after the Last Judgment. It is here that Satan and all who follow him, man and spirit alike, will be given their final judgment.

> *And the beast was taken, and with him the false prophet that wrought miracles before him, with which he deceived them that had received the mark of the beast, and them that worshipped his image. These both were cast alive into a lake of fire burning with brimstone* (Revelation 19:20).

Point: All this occurs *after* Jesus returns, so the place I experienced was not the lake, but the *hell that enlargeth itself daily*. The presence of brimstone is reserved for later. Why, God only knows. Glory to God!

CHAPTER 8

Hell Can Be Avoided

For years after this event, I continued to receive words of prophecy that I should write about my experience. I finally yielded and set out to document what I saw. Truly, others had to be warned not to choose this place. There must be a telling of the saving grace, power, and purpose of Jesus Christ. Hell can be avoided. It is His blood and death on the Cross that will rescue us from the clutches of sin, death, and hell to all those who believe.

If you have never given your life to Jesus Christ, that can change right now.

Let me share a few more facts that you should know. Hell didn't come along merely to provide a way for Jesus to scare people into believing in Him. Hell was here before Jesus was born into the earth, and He knew this.

> *For God sent not his Son into the world to condemn the world; but that the world through him might be saved* (John 3:17).

God created every person on earth with a free will. Along with that free will, every person is responsible for his/her own sinful actions in this life.

> *Behold, all souls are mine; as the soul of the father, so also the soul of the son is mine: the soul that sinneth, it shall die* (Ezekiel 18:4).

Although there are good people in the world, even the best of people have sin in their lives.

> *For all have sinned, and come short of the glory of God* (Romans 3:23).

A person's goodness cannot remove sin from his/her life. Only by accepting the solution God sent for the removal of sin, can anyone be saved from the torments of hell.

> *For God so loved the world, that he gave his only begotten Son, that whosoever believeth in Him should not perish, but have everlasting life* (John 3:16).

God gave his Son to be a substitute for you so that if you would believe on Jesus Christ's power to save you, you would not have to perish.

> *Jesus said to him, I am the way, the truth, and the life. No one comes to the Father except through Me* (John 14:6).

Jesus will save anyone who wants to be saved!

> *And it shall come to pass, that whosoever shall call on the name of the Lord shall be saved* (Acts 2:21).

In order to be saved, you must repent from your sins and believe in Jesus Christ as your Lord and Savior. In hell there are no more chances for repentance. So while the way of mercy is open, let us entreat God with a sincere heart seeking forgiveness.

> *I tell you, Nay: but, except ye repent, ye shall all likewise perish* (Luke 13:3).

If you are willing to repent, you have several things to look forward to. Every sin you have committed from the day you were born until now, will be forgiven.

> *Therefore if any man be in Christ, he is a new creature: old things are passed away; behold, all things are become new* (2 Corinthians 5:17).

Your new salvation will guarantee God's power to help you live a Christian life on earth, as well as give you access to eternal life in heaven:

> *But as many as received him, to them gave he power to become the sons of God, even to them that believe on his name* (John 1:12).

> *Verily, verily, I say unto you, He that heareth my word, and believeth on him that sent me, hath everlasting life, and shall not come into condemnation; but is passed from death unto life*
> (John 5:24).

There will be rejoicing in heaven over your decision to repent.

> *Likewise, I say unto you, there is joy in the presence of the angels of God over one sinner that repenteth* (Luke 15:10).

When you enter into heaven, you can look forward to a place where there is no more sorrow.

> *And God shall wipe away all tears from their eyes; and there shall be no more death, neither sorrow, nor crying, neither shall there be any more pain: for the former things are passed away*
> (Revelation 21:4).

Pray this prayer right now:

> *Lord, I've read this book and in my heart I acknowledge that I have sinned. I have sinned against you and others by the way I have lived and I want to change. Although I have not believed on you in the past, I don't want to face this place called hell for my future. Lord Jesus, I am sorry for the sins I have committed and with your help I will change my life and*

live for you. I ask that you come into my heart and save me. I believe you can, I believe you will, and I accept it now, in Jesus' name. Thank you, and Amen.

I encourage you to embark on a journey through the Scriptures and learn more about the glorious wonders of God in His Word. For He instructed us:

> *Thus saith the LORD, the Holy One of Israel, and his Maker, Ask me of things to come concerning my sons, and concerning the work of my hands command ye me. I have made the earth, and created man upon it: I, even my hands, have stretched out the heavens, and all their host have I commanded* (Isaiah 45:11-12).

Prepare your traveling backpack and let the study of God's Word be your next great adventure!

ENDNOTES

1. Charles G. B. Evans, *Teens and Devil Worship*, (Lafayette, LA: Huntington House Publishers, 1991), 17.
2. Lewis Drummond, *The Evangelist*, (Nashville: Thomas Nelson, 2001), 25-26.
3. Canoe.ca/indy5001997/may27_gor.html
4. http://www.chem.orst.edu/ch331-7t/ch334/MOTD928.htm
5. www.racingnewsonline.com/story.do
6. *American Heritage Dictionary of English Language, Third Edition*, (Boston: Houghton Mifflin Company, 1992).
7. Gabriele Amorth, *An Exorcist Tells His Story*, (San Francisco: Ignatius Press, 1999), 76.

Made in the USA
Monee, IL
22 February 2022